Alec Wilder

SONATA № 2

for Bassoon and Piano

Margun Music

EXCLUSIVELY DISTRIBUTED BY

HAL•LEONARD®
CORPORATION

7777 W. BLUEMOUND RD. P.O. BOX 13819 MILWAUKEE, WI 53213

COMMISSIONED BY THE NATIONAL ASSOCIATION
OF COLLEGE WIND AND PERCUSSION INSTRUCTORS

Sonata No. 2

I

ALEC WILDER

The paper used in this publication meet
the minimum requirements of America
National Standard for Information Scienc
- Permanence of Paper for Printed Librar
Materials, ANSI Z39.48-1984.

4

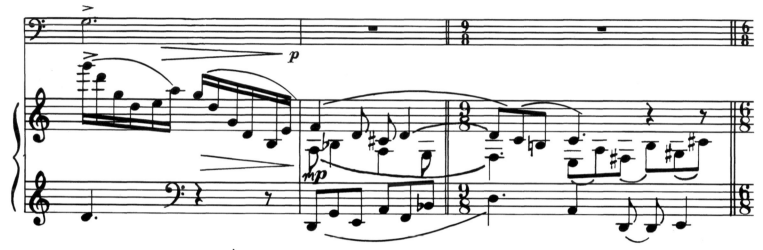

Tempo I

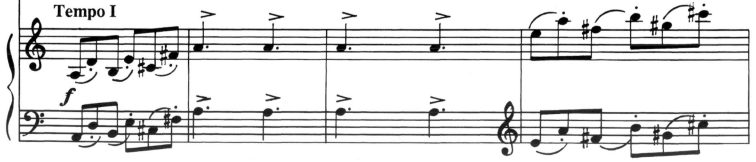

Tempo I

Tempo I

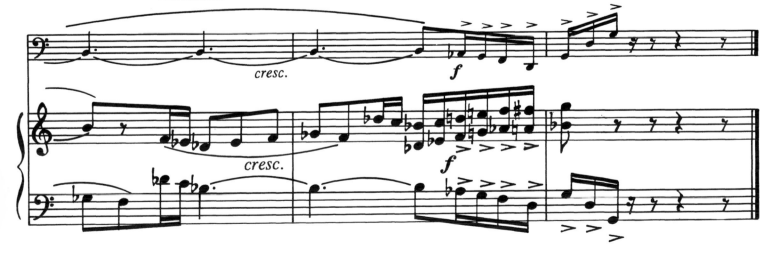

II

9

III

BASSOON

PIANO

Alec Wilder

SONATA № 2

for Bassoon and Piano

Margun Music

EXCLUSIVELY DISTRIBUTED BY

HAL•LEONARD®
CORPORATION

7777 W. BLUEMOUND RD. P.O. BOX 13819 MILWAUKEE, WI 53213

Sonata No. 2

BASSOON

ALEC WILDER

I

MM093

Meno mosso (♩. = 80)

Tempo I

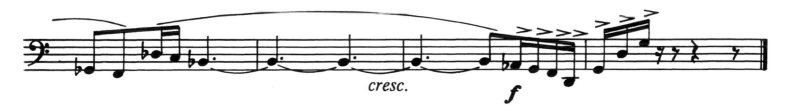

II

(Time)

8

IV

accel.

cresc.

accel.

cresc.

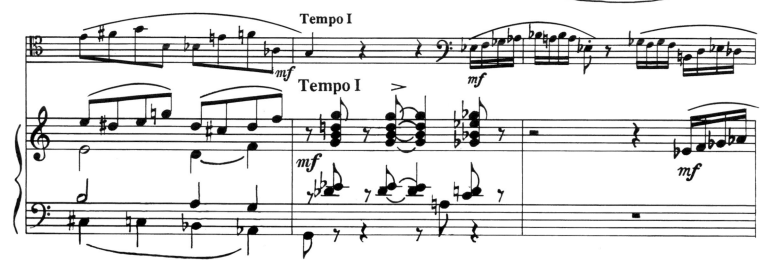

Tempo I

mf

Tempo I

mf

mf

mf

mf

18

IV

♩ = ca. 64

BASSOON

mp espr.

PIANO

mp